How the Snail Found Its Colors shows how the artist Henri Matisse used bold colors to create strikingly beautiful art. The story follows a colorless snail on a quest to find its own colors. After discovering a number of Matisse's paintings, the snail magically takes on a range of colors from the artworks.

Matisse really did create an artwork called *The Snail*. He made it in his old age, when he could no longer hold a paintbrush for long. Instead of painting a snail, he made a picture of one by sticking pieces of brightly colored paper onto canvas.

How the Snail Found Its Colors helps us understand how particular colors make us feel, and appreciate the simplicity and beauty of Matisse's amazing art.

"What fabulous colors you have!"

"Me? Fabulous? Wow!"

Original Korean text by Jeong-yi Kee and Haneul Ddang
Illustrations by Mi-ran Yang
Korean edition © Aram Publishing

This English edition published by big & SMALL in 2016
by arrangement with Aram Publishing
English text edited by Scott Forbes
English edition © big & SMALL 2016

Distributed in the United States and Canada by
Lerner Publishing Group, Inc.
241 First Avenue North
Minneapolis, MN 55401 U.S.A.
www.lernerbooks.com

ISBN: 978-1-925248-85-2

Printed in Korea

HOW THE SNAIL FOUND ITS COLORS

THE ART OF MATISSE

Written by Jeong-yi Kee and Haneul Ddang
Illustrated by Mi-ran Yang
Edited by Scott Forbes

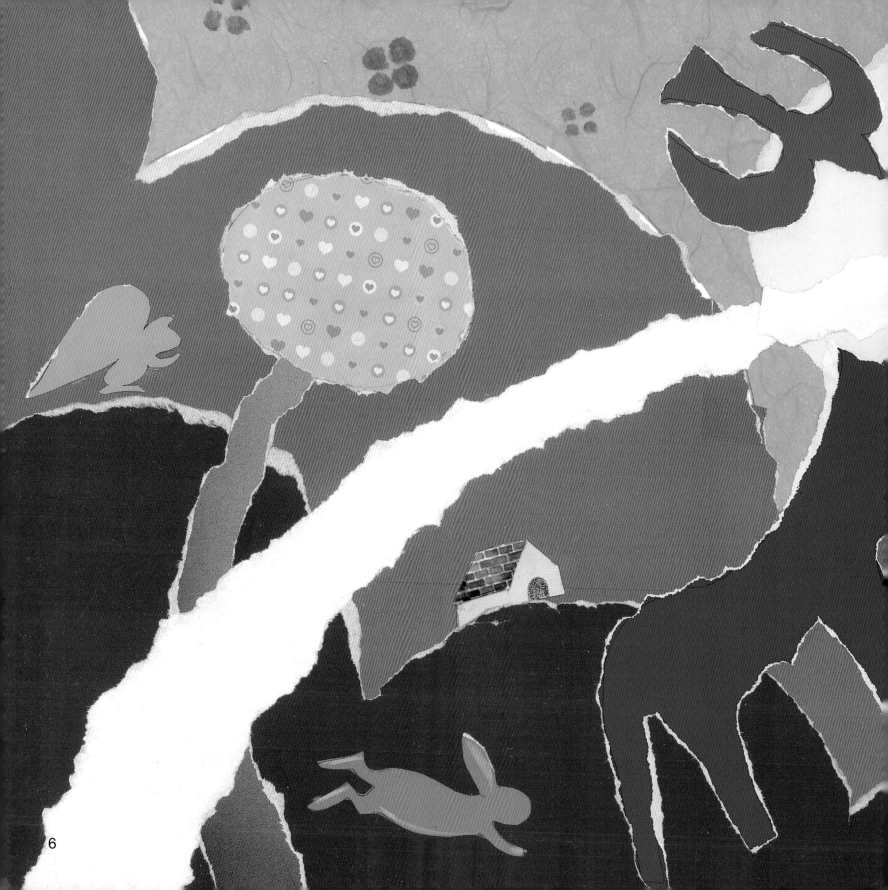

"The sun, the flowers, the insects, the sky … even the grass has its own color," said the snail.

7

"But me … I don't
have any colors."

The snail was
feeling sad.

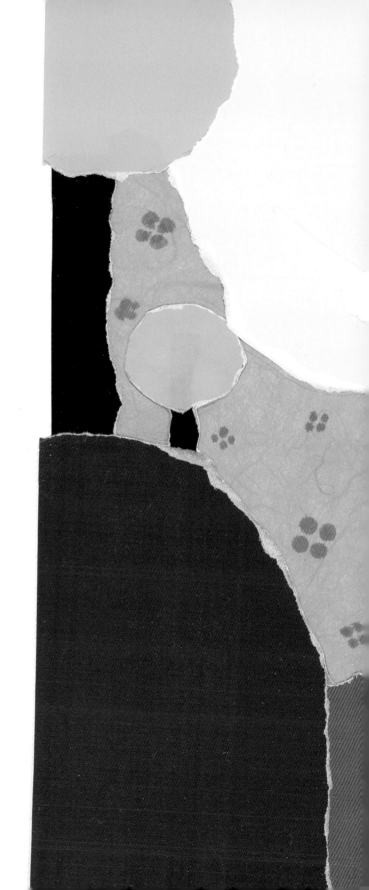

The snail wanted to become colorful too.

But how could it do that?

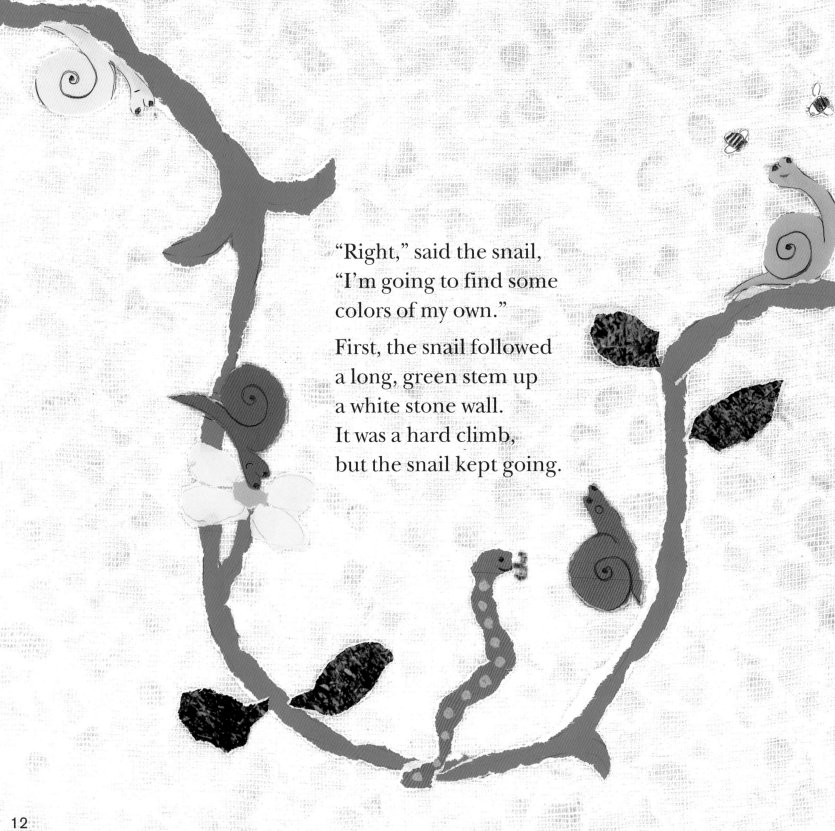

"Right," said the snail,
"I'm going to find some
colors of my own."

First, the snail followed
a long, green stem up
a white stone wall.
It was a hard climb,
but the snail kept going.

12

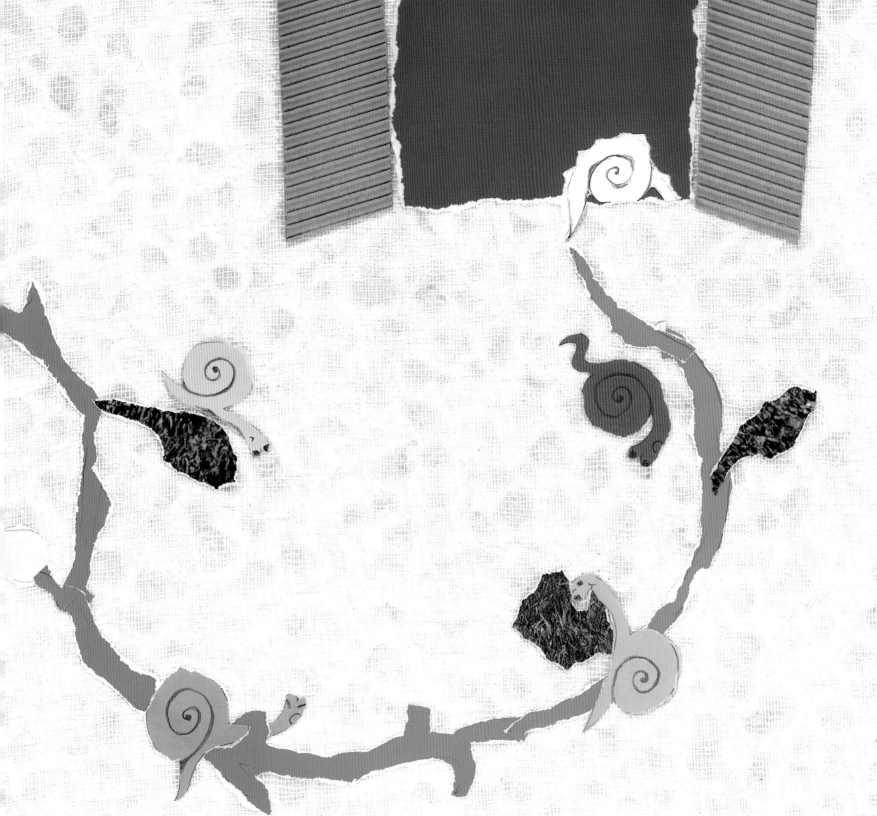

The snail entered a strange room.
It was bright red all over — above
and below and all around.
"Oh, that makes me feel lovely
and warm," said the snail.
  "I wish I could be red like this."

    The snail stayed still for a while,
      enjoying the feeling of the room.
        "Aaah," it said.

Detail from *The Red Room (Harmony in Red)* (1908), The State Hermitage Museum, St. Petersburg, Russia

15

The next room was even
more confusing.
"Which is the wall and which
is the floor?" said the snail.

Fortunately, it managed to
climb up what looked like
a bright yellow ladder
and find a way out.

Next, as the snail crossed a black floor,
soft music started playing.
When the music stopped,
the snail moved on.

It came to a place where
everything was yellow.
"Oh, that's such a soft,
soothing color," it said. "Mmm."
The snail stopped, closed its eyes,
and relaxed.

Dance (II) (1910), The Hermitage, St. Petersburg, Russia

Continuing on its way, the snail found itself surrounded by a dark blue. It really liked the color, but somehow it made the snail feel cold.

"Brr," it said, "I don't think blue is quite right for snails."

20

Music (1939), Albright-Knox Art Gallery, Buffalo, New York, USA

Soon the snail saw bright colors again and dancing figures.
"I feel like dancing too," said the snail. It stretched out its long, thin body,
and began to wriggle from side to side.
It felt its body warm up and its heart beat with excitement.

22

Suddenly, someone lifted up the snail
and said, in a soft voice,
"Oh, you are a fabulous snail."

"Me?" said the snail, "Fabulous?"
Tilting its head, it looked up
at the man who was holding it.
"Do you really think so?
But I'm just a plain, colorless snail."

"If you wait a minute,
I'll show you how wonderful
you really look," said the man.

He took up a brush
and started painting
some paper.

After he had painted several
pieces of paper in different colors,
he cut out shapes and pasted them
onto a canvas.

The Snail (1953),
Tate Modern, London, UK

"There you are," the old man said,
and he held up the picture proudly.

The snail was beside itself with joy.
"Is that really me?" it asked.
The old man nodded.
The snail smiled back at him.
"Then I really am a fabulous snail!"

H. Matisse
53

29

A magician with colors

Matisse in his old age

Henri Matisse was born in France in 1869. In his early years he showed little interest in art and his first job was as a lawyer. But then he became sick and couldn't work for a while. During this period he began drawing and painting and found that he loved it.

From that day on, Matisse wanted to become a painter. His father was strongly against this idea, but Matisse enrolled in an art school in Paris and began to study painting. Unfortunately his teachers didn't think much of his work and paid him little attention. Matisse looked for another teacher who would recognize his talents, and soon he found one: a famous artist called Gustave Moreau.

Learning the basics

Moreau taught Matisse to go back to basics. He told him to study the works of earlier painters and re-learn the skills needed for painting. So Matisse went to the Louvre Museum in Paris and practiced copying famous artworks.

Matisse wasn't a genius who produced amazing paintings without any instruction. It took him time to perfect his skills and develop his own unique style. But once he did, he quickly found fame. Another famous artist, Pablo Picasso, said Matisse was a "magician" with colors.

1869	1887	1889	1890	1892	1905
Born in December 31, in Le Cateau, Picardy, France	After finishing high school, Matisse studies law at the University of Paris	Works at the Deconseille law firm	While resting after an operation, decides to become a painter	Enrols in art school in Paris and takes lessons with Gustave Moreau	Works appear in exhibition of the Fauves in Paris

Wild art

Matisse learned how to use colors partly by studying modern painters such as Paul Gauguin and Vincent Van Gogh. When Matisse first saw Gauguin's paintings, he was astonished by their use of bright primary colors — red, blue, and yellow. Matisse felt that strong colors were more important than making paintings realistic, and he began to use primary colors in many of his works. Some people thought the paintings were wild. As a result, Matisse and other painters who used a similar style became known as the "wild beasts," or *fauves* in French.

Matisse and André Derain are the best known of the Fauves. They both used strong brushwork and vivid colors to express emotions. The Fauves influenced many other painters. A group called the Expressionists adopted a similar approach, for example. But their paintings included even more distorted shapes and usually had more serious themes. One of the most famous Expressionist artists is the Norwegian painter Edvard Munch.

Music (1939), Albright-Knox Art Gallery, Buffalo, New York, USA

Portrait of Vlaminck (1905) by André Derain, Musée de l'Annonciade, Saint-Tropez, France

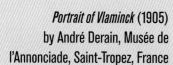

The Scream (1893) by Edvard Munch, National Gallery, Oslo, Norway

1908
Works exhibited in Germany, Russia, and the United States

1918
Exhibits alongside Pablo Picasso at the Paul Guillaume Gallery, Paris

1947
Creates illustrations for *The Flowers of Evil*, a book by French poet Charles Baudelaire

1948
Designs Chapel of the Rosary, in Vence, France

1951
Completes Chapel of the Rosary

1954
Dies in Nice, France

Colors and emotions

Matisse believed expressing emotion in painting was more important than painting realistically. One way to achieve that was to use bright colors. His success allowed other artists to try similar things.

Take a closer look at Matisse's painting *The Red Room*. It shows a bright red room and, outside, green fields, yellow flowers, and blue sky. But it's the blue patterns on the studio walls and tablecloth that hold our attention. Because the walls and the floor are the same color, you don't get a sense of space. You can't tell how much space there is, for example, between the wall and the table.

The Red Room (Harmony in Red) (1908), The State Hermitage Museum, St. Petersburg, Russia

Matisse painted *Dance (II)* for a Russian businessman and art collector, Sergei Shchukin. It is one of his most joyful artworks and that feeling is expressed mainly by the strong colors.

Dance (II) (1910), The State Hermitage Museum, St. Petersburg, Russia

Simpler, bolder, and stronger

By the early 1960s, Matisse was an old man and quite weak. He found it difficult to hold a paintbrush for long spells. But he still wanted to create art. So he developed a new method of working. He quickly painted sheets of paper in different colors. Then he cut the pieces of paper into shapes and pasted them onto a canvas. These works were simpler – but also bolder and more vivid – than his paintings.

Twenty years after Matisse painted *Dance (II)*, a famous art collector called Alfred Barnes asked him to paint a similar work for the walls of his gallery. It was too hard for Matisse to paint directly onto the walls, so Barnes sent a giant canvas to France for Matisse to work on. Matisse used cut-out shapes to plan the giant painting, called *The Dance II*, which he completed in 1932.

The Snail (1953), Tate Modern, London, UK

Study for *The Dance II* (1932), Barnes Foundation, Philadelphia, USA

"Are these really my colors? …

They're so beautiful!"